THE ART
OF
PERSUASION

Winning Over Your Audience

Pius Borr

TABLE OF CONTENTS

INTRODUCTION

Anybody who wishes to succeed in today's world, both personally and professionally, must possess the capacity to persuade others. The skill of persuasion is the key to attaining your goals, whether you're attempting to persuade your employer to give you a promotion, persuade a potential customer to do business with you, or simply make a strong case in a debate.

A thorough manual that will teach you everything you need to know to master persuasion is The Art of Persuasion: How to Win Over Any Audience.

This book will give you the methods and tools you need to establish rapport with your audience, connect with them on a personal level, and convey messages that are compelling enough to elicit action. It does this by drawing on the most recent findings in psychology, communication, and neuroscience.

You will learn how to determine your audience's needs, design your message for optimum impact, and employ persuasion through language and nonverbal cues through practical exercises and real-world situations.

Also, you will learn how to get through typical deterrents to persuasion like resistance, skepticism, and objections and use them as chances to support your case.

The Art of Persuasion will offer you the abilities and self-assurance you need to persuade any audience, whether you are a seasoned public speaker, a salesperson trying to close more transactions, or simply someone who wants to be more effective in their everyday encounters. Let's dive in and learn more about the power of persuasion, shall we?

CHAPTER 1

UNDERSTANDING THE PSYCHOLOGY OF PERSUASION

Persuasion is an art, but it's also a science In this chapter, we'll examine the core ideas of persuasion and how to apply them to persuade any audience.

Understanding the psychology of persuasion is essential for achieving your goals, whether you're attempting to persuade a group of investors to fund your startup or convincing your employer to give you a promotion.

Trustworthiness and Social Evidence

Credibility is the fundamental rule of persuasion. Credibility is the idea that other people have of you that you are reliable and knowledgeable about a given topic.

Someone who is believable in the eyes of the audience has a better chance of convincing them. You need knowledge, experience, and a proven track record of achievement to establish your reputation.

Social proof is the second persuasive principle. The concept of social proof holds that people are more likely to imitate their like-minded peers. Someone who shares their values and ideas has a greater chance of influencing people. Building a relationship with your audience and becoming familiar with their needs and issues is necessary to establish social proof.

Moral Arguments

Emotional appeals are the third rule of persuasive communication. Decision-making is heavily influenced by emotions, and messages that arouse powerful emotions are more persuasive.

One way to make an emotional appeal is to emphasize the advantages of your idea, play on your audience's sense of urgency, or establish a personal connection with them.

Preventing Common Errors

When attempting to convince others, people frequently make a number of blunders. Neglecting to take your audience's viewpoint into account is one of the most frequent errors.

Crafting a persuasive message that appeals to your audience requires having a thorough understanding of their needs and values. Using jargon or technical language that your audience might not understand is another common error.

Clear, concise, and simple-to-understand language is necessary for effective communication.

Credibility and social proof are crucial for establishing your authority in your profession as well as for influencing your audience.

It's crucial to establish a reputation for credibility and social proof if you want to be recognized as a thought leader or an authority in your field. This can be accomplished through building a strong web presence, producing thought-provoking content, and giving presentations at trade shows.

Although they can be a potent weapon for persuasion, emotional appeals must be used with caution. You don't want to sound fake or try to trick your audience. Instead, concentrate on employing sincere and genuine emotional appeals. If you're attempting to convince your supervisor to promote you, for instance, you might mention how enthusiastic you are about your work and how hard you've been working to advance your talents.

Focusing too much on one's own needs and interests when trying to persuade others is another typical error. It's important to concentrate on your audience's needs and desires if you want to persuade them.

You must comprehend their concerns and how your suggestion might assist in resolving them. You may make your message more engaging and persuasive by framing it in a way that responds to the needs and desires of your audience.

everybody who wishes to succeed in their personal and professional lives must understand the psychology of persuasion. You can develop persuading messages that motivate action by establishing credibility and social proof, employing emotional appeals, and concentrating on the needs and wants of your audience.

CHAPTER 2

UNDERSTANDING YOUR AUDIENCE

Your audience's needs, attitudes, and beliefs must be understood if you want to persuade them. This chapter looks at how to frame your message for optimum impact and how to determine the requirements and values of your audience.

Identifying Your Audience

Discovering your audience's identity is the first step towards understanding them. Both their psychographic information—such as their hobbies, values, and beliefs and their demographic information such as their age, gender, and location are included in this. You may adapt your message to their unique wants and preferences by being aware of the demographic and psychographic characteristics of your audience.

How to Frame Your Message

It's critical to communicate in a way that resonates with your audience once you've determined who they are. In order to do this, you should speak in simple, understandable language and use relatable examples and tales. Along with these factors, keep in mind the media via which you will deliver your message as well as its tone and style.

Finding Common Ground with Your Audience

Using your audience's values is among the most powerful strategies for persuasion. People utilize values as their compass while making decisions and figuring out how to live in the world.

You may craft a message that resonates to the hearts and minds of your audience by being aware of their values.

As an illustration, you may appeal to the sustainability and conservation ideals of an environmentalist group to get their support for your project.

You might highlight how your project is planned to decrease waste and reduce carbon footprint, and how it ties in with their principles of environmental protection.

Use of Statistics and Data

Using statistics and facts is a further powerful technique to influence your audience. Facts and statistics offer unbiased support for your arguments, can help you establish your credibility as an expert on a subject, and can also be used to promote your message.

Data and statistics should be used wisely and with caution, though. Don't overburden your audience with information; instead, make sure that the material you use is reliable and pertinent to them.

Message Customization for Various Audiences

You might need to adjust your message depending on the audience you're speaking to because not all audiences are created equally. For instance, you might need to emphasize the financial implications of your plan if you're presenting to a group of executives.

On the other hand, if you're addressing a group of employees, you might need to concentrate more on how your suggestion will impact their regular work.

It's critical to conduct advance audience research to successfully adapt your messaging. Get details regarding their job responsibilities, top priorities, and trouble spots. You can choose the most effective approach to frame your message for greatest impact using the information provided.

Cultural Differences to Be Understood

Consideration of cultural differences is another crucial component of audience comprehension. In one culture, what might be convincing might not be as powerful in another.

For example, before concluding a corporate agreement, it could be more crucial in some cultures to build a personal bond. The importance of providing data and statistics to support your argument may differ depending on the culture.

It's critical to conduct thorough research before speaking to a group of people from a foreign culture. Make your message more appropriate by being familiar with their traditions, beliefs, and communication methods.

Intuition and Active Listening

You need to work on your empathy and active listening skills in order to genuinely comprehend your audience. By doing this, you must strive to place yourself in their position and view the world from their viewpoint.

It also entails paying close attention to how they speak and behave and then responding appropriately.

Your audience may be more open to your message if you practice empathy and active listening since you will have established trust and connection with them.

To develop communications that persuade and motivate action, it is crucial to comprehend your audience. You may make your message more persuasive and effective by adapting it to diverse audiences, taking cultural variations into account, and engaging in active listening and empathy exercises.

In the following chapter, we'll discuss using narrative to craft a message that draws in your audience and motivates them to act.

CHAPTER 3

UNDERSTANDING THE PSYCHOLOGY OF PERSUASION

The psychological method of persuasion involves appealing to the emotions, beliefs, and values of your audience. This chapter will examine the main psychological concepts that support persuasive communication and show you how to apply them to persuade any audience.

The Influence of Feeling

Emotion is one of the most effective persuasion tactics. By appealing to the emotions of your audience, you can craft a message that is more captivating and convincing. Emotions are powerful motivators of action and decision-making.

You need to know what matters to and drives your audience in order to appeal to their emotions. Understanding their values, beliefs, and interests will help you accomplish this.

You can craft a message that appeals directly to your audience's emotions once you know what drives them.

Considering Cognitive Bias

Our brains use cognitive biases, which are mental short cuts, to hasten decision-making. These biases have the potential to affect our perceptions and actions in ways that we aren't always conscious of. It's critical for persuaders to comprehend these biases and how they may affect the choices made by their audiences.

For instance, the confirmation bias is a propensity to dismiss information that contradicts our ideas in favor of information that supports our current opinions.

You might need to give information that contradicts your audience's presumptions and preconceptions in order to overcome this prejudice.

Social Support and Power

The use of social proof and authority is an important component of persuasion. The concept of "social proof" holds that people are more likely to act in accordance with the crowd. On the other side, authority is the notion that people are more likely to pay attention to someone who is seen as an authority or expert on a subject.

You might need to include testimonials, case studies, or expert endorsements in your persuasive communications if you want to capitalize on social proof and authority. You can raise the likelihood that your audience will be persuaded by demonstrating that others have already adopted the action you're suggesting or by building your own authority.

The Function of Mutuality

The notion of reciprocity holds that people are obligated to return a favor or act of kindness. You can engender a sense of oweness in your audience by doing something for them, which may increase their receptivity to your message.

You may, for instance, give away a sample of your good or service to your audience, or you could provide them useful knowledge. By giving something of value, you foster a sense of reciprocity that may make them more open to your message.

It's necessary to realize that people frequently base their decisions on their intuition or "gut emotions" in order to better comprehend the function of psychology in persuasion. Heuristics enter the picture in this situation.

We employ heuristics mental short cuts to make decisions fast, frequently without fully taking into account all of the facts at hand.

You can modify your persuasive message to appeal to your audience's decision-making processes by being aware of the potential heuristics they may utilize.

For instance, the availability heuristic is the propensity to base decisions on information that is easily accessible. In order to sway this heuristic, you could offer instances or anecdotes that highlight the advantages of performing the suggested action.

The anchoring effect is another heuristic, which is the propensity to overly depend on the first piece of information a decision-maker encounters. You might need to offer a number of pieces of evidence that counteract this bias in order to convince the reader of your position.

It's crucial to take into account how emotions affect decision-making. According to research, people tend to base their decisions on their emotional responses to a scenario before using logic to support those conclusions later.

You may create a convincing message that appeals to your audience's emotions and increases the likelihood of success by understanding the emotional factors that influence your audience's decision-making.

Ultimately, creating persuasive messages that connect with your audience requires an understanding of the psychology of persuasion. You can craft a message that is more compelling and successful by making use of emotions, cognitive biases, heuristics, and other psychological concepts.

For persuasive communications to be effective, it is crucial to comprehend the psychology of persuasion. You can craft a message that is more persuasive and powerful by appealing to your audience's emotions, comprehending cognitive biases, utilizing social proof and authority, and applying reciprocity. The use of visual aids to strengthen your persuasive message and improve your chances of success.

CHAPTER 4

DEVELOPING CREDIBILITY AND TRUST

Building credibility and trust is essential for persuasion. Individuals are more likely to be convinced by someone they believe to be credible and trustworthy.

In this chapter, we'll look at ways to boost the persuasiveness of your messaging by establishing credibility and trust with your audience.

Setting Up Your Expertise

By demonstrating your knowledge of the subject at issue, you can establish credibility with your audience. This can be accomplished by demonstrating your credentials, expertise, or subject understanding.

You might emphasize your industry expertise, any prior profitable businesses you've led, any accolades or prizes you've won, for instance, if you're trying to convince a group of investors to support your startup.

Giving Examples and Support

By offering proof and instances to back up your claims, you can also increase your audience's perception of your credibility.

This might show that your message is supported by data and facts rather than just your opinion or personal convictions.

You may use research reports, market statistics, or expert comments as proof. You could also give examples and case studies to demonstrate why the course of action you suggest is advantageous.

Being open-minded and truthful

Honesty and transparency are also crucial components in winning over your audience's trust. You risk losing the audience's trust if you are not open and honest about your intentions as well as any dangers or disadvantages associated with your proposal.

Being open and truthful about your goals and the possible results of performing the proposed action is necessary to establish trust. This entails being honest about any conflicts of interest or biases you may have, as well as any potential downsides or hazards.

Developing Personal Relationships

Establishing a personal rapport with your audience can help to boost trust and the potency of your persuasive message.

You may make your audience more responsive to your message and improve their chances of being convinced by building connection with them.

You can utilize humor or other forms of entertainment to interest your audience, or you can share personal anecdotes or stories that are relevant to the topic at hand. To foster a sense of community, you may also strive to connect with your audience through similar experiences or interests.

There are a few additional methods you can use in addition to the ones previously discussed to establish credibility and trust with your audience.

Establishing a common ground with your audience is crucial first. You can show that you comprehend their viewpoint and are able to relate to their issues by discovering comparable experiences or hobbies.

This can increase trust among your audience members and increase their openness to your message.

Being consistent with your message and behavior is another method to gain respect and trust. Your audience can view you as unreliable or untrustworthy if you say one thing and do another. You may show your integrity and win the audience's trust by being consistent in your words and deeds.

It's critical to treat your audience with respect and courtesy. It's crucial to accept and recognize others' points of view, even if you disagree with their beliefs or viewpoints.

You may develop trust and a good relationship with your audience by treating them with respect. It's crucial to take into account your nonverbal communication when trying to establish credibility and trust. Your voice and body language can say a lot about your honesty and credibility.

Maintaining eye contact with your audience, for instance, might help to build rapport and project confidence. In a similar vein, speaking clearly and authoritatively can help to demonstrate your subject-matter knowledge and competence.

It's also critical to be conscious of your body language and facial expressions. Avoiding closed-off or defensive postures, such as crossing your arms, will enable you to come off to your audience as open and responsive.

Being well-prepared and organized when presenting is another approach to gain respect and trust. This can show your knowledge and care for the little things. Your message will be more persuasive and help to establish your credibility if it is concise and well-organized.

Ultimately, it's critical to exercise patience as you develop your audience's credibility and confidence. It takes time and constant work to establish trust.

You may progressively develop trust and credibility over time by continually demonstrating your subject matter expertise, offering arguments and examples, being open and truthful, and forming connections with your audience on a human level.

Establishing trust and credibility is a key component of persuasive communication. You may improve the impact of your persuasive message and persuade even the most resistant audiences by establishing your expertise, offering proof and examples, being open and honest, and developing personal connections with your audience.

CHAPTER 5

POWER OF STORYTELLING IN PERSUASIVE COMMUNICATION

Storytelling is an effective method of persuasion. Using storytelling to engage your audience and make your point more remembered can be useful when trying to sell a product, convince someone to take action, or alter someone's mind.

Storytelling is powerful because it can emote your audience, which is one of the reasons it works so well. You may establish empathy and a connection with your audience by narrating a tale. This can boost the likelihood that your audience will remember and take action on your message by making it more personal and meaningful.

Furthermore, narrative can aid in the simplification of complex concepts and increase audience accessibility.

You can aid in simplifying and improving the understanding of complex subjects by using approachable characters and tangible examples. This can strengthen your message's persuasiveness and raise the chance that your audience will accept it as true.

Using storytelling to engage and keep your audience's attention is another advantage. A well-told story can be engrossing and interesting, keeping your audience's attention and interested in your message. This can improve the impact of your persuasive message and raise the likelihood that your audience will act.

A few things should be kept in mind while employing narrative in persuasive communication. Choosing the appropriate tale for your audience and message comes first.

The narrative should aid to illustrate the argument you are attempting to make and should be pertinent, relatable, and interesting.

Second, it's critical to strategically employ storytelling. Instead of detracting from your key arguments, the tale should be incorporated into your message in a way that supports and strengthens them. It is critical to develop and improve your storytelling abilities. As with any skill, storytelling requires practice and criticism to perfect.

You may increase your audience connection and the impact of your persuasive message by honing your storytelling skills and seeking feedback from others.

Narrative is an effective technique for persuasion. You can make your persuasive message more memorable and impactful by connecting with your audience on an emotional level, demystifying difficult concepts, grabbing and holding their attention, and strategically leveraging narrative.

The importance of emotion in persuasive communication

Emotions are a crucial component of persuasive communication because they affect how messages are understood and acted upon.

Messages that are emotionally charged are more likely to capture an audience's attention, provoke a strong response, and eventually change behavior.

The ability of emotions to be more memorable than other modes of communication is one of the reasons why they are so effective in persuading.

According to research, when people are given knowledge, material that elicits a strong emotional response is more likely to stick in their memories than information that is neutral. To ensure that their message is not only heard but also remembered, persuaders must use emotional appeals in their communications.

Fear, wrath, excitement, and sadness are just a few of the emotional arguments that persuaders can employ to connect with their audience. A message can be used to affect how an audience perceives and responds to one of these emotions.

For instance, fear can be a strong motivator. Persuaders can instill a sense of urgency in their audience and motivate them to act by emphasizing the detrimental effects of inaction. This is frequently observed in advertising campaigns that make use of fright appeals to persuade people to take action to safeguard their safety or health.

Another emotion that works well in persuasive communication is anger. People are more likely to act to solve the problem that is making them upset while they are angry.

By spotlighting a problem that would likely make their audience upset and outlining a workable remedy, persuaders can capitalize on this feeling.

Emotional arguments based on happiness and joy are very powerful. Positive emotions seem to make people more receptive to novel concepts and viewpoints. To evoke these feelings and foster a more favorable relationship with their message, persuaders can utilize comedy, narrative, inspirational pictures and videos.

An effective emotional appeal can also be sadness, especially when aiming to generate compassion and understanding. Persuaders can elicit an emotional response that can motivate action by emphasizing the troubles or difficulties that others encounter.

This is frequently employed in fundraising drives to draw attention to the condition of people or animals in need.

It's crucial to remember that emotional appeals must be handled morally and sensibly. It's important for persuaders to be aware of the possibility of manipulating or abusing emotions for their own benefit.

Although they can be an effective weapon for persuasion, emotions must be handled with caution and concern for the listener.

Compelling communication depends heavily on emotions. An audience's attention can be captured, communications can be made more memorable, and behavior can ultimately be affected via emotional appeals.

Persuaders can create messages that resonate with their audience and motivate action by understanding the various emotional appeals and employing them sensibly.

CHAPTER 6

FRAMING YOUR MESSAGE FOR MAXIMUM IMPACT

An essential component of compelling communication is framing your message. Your audience's perception of your message and the success of your persuasive communication can both be impacted by how you frame your message.

Understanding your audience is a key component in framing your message. You may make your message more compelling and persuasive by tailoring it to your audience's values, beliefs, and interests. For instance, it might be more beneficial to frame your message around the environmental advantages of your product or service than to emphasize cost savings if you are attempting to persuade a group of environmentalists.

Making the appropriate word and phrase choices is another component of framing your message.

Your audience's perception of your message may be influenced by the language you use. For instance, using positive language can foster optimism and hope, but using negative language might foster fear and apprehension.

Making your message memorable and compelling can also be accomplished by using vivid language and metaphors.

Also, framing your message may entail emphasizing the advantages while downplaying the disadvantages.

This can be done by employing strategies including emphasizing the special qualities and advantages of your good or service, contrasting it with rivals, and showing the prospective advantages of taking action.

Taking into account the context in which your message is being delivered is also crucial. Your message's delivery and context can affect how it is received and how much of an impact it has.

Delivering a message, for instance, after a project is completed or during a celebratory event can help to boost the effect of your message because these times are when your audience is most receptive and engaged.

Using social evidence can also help frame your message and boost its effect. Build credibility and trust with your audience by employing endorsements or testimonials from pleased clients or other reputable figures. This might make your message more persuasive by raising its perceived worth.

Message framing is an essential component of persuasive communication, to sum up. You can improve the impact and efficacy of your message by knowing your audience, using appropriate language, highlighting benefits, taking the situation into account, and utilizing social proof.

Knowing the underlying values and beliefs of your audience is another crucial component of framing your message.

You may craft your message to more deeply connect with your audience by being aware of what matters to them and what drives them. For instance, if your target audience cares about sustainability, you might frame your message to emphasize the advantages of your product or service for the environment.

Additionally, framing your message may involve the use of persuasion strategies like anchoring, in which you tie your message to a particular point of reference to affect how your audience interprets it. For instance, to make your product appear more affordable, you could base its price on a more expensive comparable item.

Addressing potential objections or worries that your audience may have can also be a part of framing your message. You may raise the perceived worth of your message and help to establish trust by recognizing and responding to potential objections.

Using visual aids or other multimedia components to strengthen your message and raise its impact is another way to frame your message. A graph or chart, for instance, might help to make your message more memorable and understandable by visually representing facts.

Last but not least, it's critical to be conscious of any biases or preconceptions that might exist among your audience. You may maximize the impact of your message and raise your chances of success by being aware of and addressing these prejudices.

Overall, understanding your audience, selecting the appropriate words and phrases, presenting your message in a way that highlights benefits, addressing objections and concerns, using persuasive techniques, and being conscious of biases and preconceptions are all important components of framing your message for maximum impact.

You may improve the impact of your persuasive communication and get the results you want by following these steps.

CHAPTER 7

USING EMOTIONAL APPEALS TO CONNECT WITH YOUR AUDIENCE

An effective technique to engage your audience and leave a lasting impression is by using emotional appeals.

By appealing to your audience's emotions, you can influence their behavior. Emotions can affect how we make decisions.

Telling your audience relatable stories is one method to employ emotional appeals. By appealing to the emotions and values of your audience, stories can help you connect with them on an emotional level. In order to elicit an emotional response from your audience, you can employ vivid language and images when telling a tale. This may aid in capturing their attention and helping them remember your message.

Appealing to the values and beliefs of your audience is another technique to employ emotional appeals.

You may craft your message to more deeply connect with your audience by learning about the values and ideas that are significant to them.

For instance, you might utilize language and imagery that recalls the ideals of family and community to establish an emotional connection with your audience.

Another effective strategy for engaging your audience on an emotional level is through comedy. Your audience will be more receptive to your message if you use humor to help them feel good. But it's crucial to employ humor in a way that suits your target audience and complements the general tone of your message.

Also, adding visual aids and other multimedia components might help you engage your audience on an emotional level. For instance, presenting pictures or films that arouse a particular feeling might support your point and leave a lasting impact.

Finally, when making emotional appeals, it's critical to be genuine. If you are being manipulative or fake, your audience will be able to tell, which will damage your credibility and weaken your message.

Being sincere and open can help you forge a deeper emotional bond with your listeners and improve the impact of your message.

In conclusion, appealing to your audience's emotions is a potent technique to engage them and urge them to act.

You can build a strong emotional bond with your audience and get the results you want by sharing stories, appealing to values and beliefs, using humor, using visual aids, being sincere, and being open and honest.

The role of body language in persuasive communication
Body language is important in persuasive communication because it can persuade

your audience of important ideas without using words. Your audience will form an opinion of you based on how you hold yourself, make motions, and display your face.

Confidence is among the most crucial elements of body language in compelling communication. To project confidence and authority, stand tall, make eye contact, and use open gestures.

Your credibility will rise as a result, and your audience will be more receptive to your message.

Mirroring is another crucial component of body language. Mirroring entails mimicking your audience's body language, which can promote rapport and connection. To show that you are involved and interested in what your audience is saying, you can, for instance, lean forward if they are.

Another effective approach to emphasize your points and reinforce your message is through hand gestures. Yet, it's crucial to employ gestures in a way that feels genuine and natural rather than forced or overdone.

Another crucial component of body language in persuasive communication is facial expressions. Your facial expressions can assist you communicate emotion and show how you are feeling about what you are saying.

A smile, for instance, can imply friendliness and warmth, whilst a brow wrinkle can imply worry or seriousness.

In addition to these nonverbal indicators, the tone of your voice can accentuate certain parts of your message and express emotion.

Changing up your tone and pitch might assist you keep your audience interested and emphasize how important your message is.

Generally, compelling communication relies heavily on body language. You may boost the effectiveness of your message and influence your audience to act by expressing confidence, mirroring your audience, employing natural hand gestures, using the right facial expressions, and changing your tone of voice.

The significance of attentive listening in persuasive communication.

Active listening is a crucial component of persuasive communication, as it allows the speaker to better understand their audience and tailor their message to their needs and concerns.

In this article, we will explore the importance of active listening in persuasive communication and provide tips on how to improve your listening skills.

First, it is important to understand what active listening is. Active listening involves giving your full attention to the speaker, both verbally and nonverbally. This means making eye contact, nodding your head to show you are listening, and providing verbal cues such as "I understand" or "I see." Active listening also involves asking clarifying questions and reflecting back what the speaker has said to ensure you have understood their message correctly.

Active listening is important in persuasive communication for several reasons. First, it allows the speaker to understand the concerns and needs of their audience.

This enables the speaker to tailor their message to address these concerns and make it more relevant to their audience. For example, if the audience is concerned about the environmental impact of a product, the speaker can focus on the product's sustainability features.

Second, active listening helps build rapport and trust between the speaker and the audience. By showing that you are fully engaged and interested in what the audience has to say, you demonstrate that you value their opinions and are willing to listen to their perspective.

This can help to build a relationship of trust and respect, which is essential in persuasive communication.

Third, active listening helps to prevent misunderstandings and miscommunication. By asking clarifying questions and reflecting back what the speaker has said, you can ensure that you have understood their message correctly. This can help to prevent misunderstandings and ensure that your message is accurately received and understood by your audience.

So, how can you improve your active listening skills? Here are a few tips:

Focus on the speaker: When listening to someone, focus your attention solely on them. Avoid distractions such as checking your phone or looking around the room.

Show that you are listening: Make eye contact with the speaker and use verbal cues such as "I see" or "I understand" to show that you are engaged and interested.

Ask clarifying questions: If you are unsure about something the speaker has said, ask them to clarify. This can help to prevent misunderstandings and ensure that you have understood their message correctly.

Reflect back what the speaker has said: Repeat back what the speaker has said in your own words to ensure that you have understood their message correctly.

Active listening is a critical component of persuasive communication. By showing that you are fully engaged and interested in what the audience has to say, you can build rapport and trust, better understand their needs and concerns, and prevent misunderstandings.

By following the tips outlined above, you can improve your active listening skills and become a more effective persuasive communicator.

CHAPTER 8

THE POWER OF NONVERBAL COMMUNICATION

It's not just what you say that matters when it comes to persuasive communication; it's also how you say it. Your audience's perception of your message can be significantly influenced by nonverbal cues including body language, facial expressions, and tone of voice.

Body language is among the most significant elements of nonverbal communication. Important messages can be conveyed to your audience by your posture, gestures, and facial expressions. Standing tall and making eye contact, for instance, might project confidence and authority, whereas crossing one's arms or slouching can express defensiveness or lack of interest.

One other significant component of nonverbal communication is gestures. Key ideas can be emphasized and visual attention for your audience can be generated through the use of hand movements.

Yet, it's crucial to employ gestures in a way that feels organic and genuine rather than forced or overdone.

In nonverbal communication, facial expressions are equally crucial. Your facial expressions can be used to portray emotion and show how you are feeling about a message. For instance, a smile might indicate friendliness and warmth, whereas a brow wrinkle can indicate worry or seriousness.

Voice inflection is yet another crucial component of nonverbal communication. It's possible that how you say something matters just as much as what you say.

By changing your voice and pitch, you can keep your audience interested and accentuate important parts of your message.

In general, nonverbal cues can have a significant impact on persuasive communication. Your message will be more powerful and your audience will be more likely to act if you project confidence through your body language, natural hand movements, proper facial emotions, and a variety of voice tones.

Furthermore, it's critical to consider how various audiences and cultural contexts might interpret your nonverbal cues. It's crucial to be aware of cultural variations and adapt your communication style accordingly.

For example, various cultures may have different standards and expectations about body language and tone of voice.

Persuasive communication depends heavily on knowing your audience. You must be aware of what inspires and connects with the person you are trying to influence. This entails spending time learning about and researching the wants, desires, and morals of your audience.

Doing study prior to communicating is one technique to comprehend your audience. This could entail conducting surveys or focus groups, looking at demographic data, or examining social media involvement.

You can make adjustments to your message to make it more resonant with your audience by being aware of their interests and preferences.

Active listening during your speech is a further strategy for comprehending your audience. Take attention to their responses and feedback, then modify your message as necessary. You might need to simplify your message or provide more background, for instance, if you observe that your audience is uninterested or perplexed.

Use language and examples that your target audience will comprehend and be able to relate to when customizing your message for them.

Keep your audience in mind when employing technical phrases or industry-specific jargon. Instead, utilize plain, succinct, and understandable language.

Consider the emotional appeals that will connect with your audience the greatest as well. This can entail identifying the problems or difficulties that your target audience is now encountering and then providing answers that can allay those worries. As an alternative, you can concentrate on the advantages and gains that your audience can anticipate from adopting your suggestions.

You must approach your communication with empathy and authenticity in order to properly connect with your audience. Be sincere in your communication and demonstrate real concern for your audience's needs and interests.

You can boost the likelihood that your message will persuade your audience by developing trust and rapport with them.

Use of visual aids and other supporting resources in persuasive communication

You can greatly improve your persuasive communication by using visual aids and other supporting materials. These resources can be used effectively to support your arguments, give context, and explain your claims.

The presentation slide is one of the most widely used types of visual aids. It's crucial to maintain your presentation's slides straightforward, understandable, and visually appealing.

Keep your slides from becoming overly text- or image-heavy. Use images that are directly related to your message and that support your views instead.

Case studies and real-world examples are another powerful technique for persuasion in communication. You can help establish credibility and raise the possibility that your audience will be persuaded by giving specific examples of how your message has worked in practice.

It's crucial to think about your message's tone and delivery in addition to visual aids. In addition to being personable and relatable, your tone should be assured and authoritative.

Adopt a conversational tone, and make sure to give your speech lots of pauses and breaks so that your audience can fully comprehend what you're saying.

Last but not least, practice your speech before giving your presentation. Try to foresee any queries or worries that your audience might have as you practice your speech several times.

This will make sure that you are well-prepared and self-assured when you give your message.

You may strengthen the effect of your persuasive communication and raise the probability that your audience will be persuaded by adopting a strategic approach to your visual aids, tone, and delivery.

CHAPTER 9

MASTERING BODY LANGUAGE AND VOICE

Successful persuasive communication involves more than simply your words; it also involves your delivery. In this chapter, we'll look at how to control your voice and body language to make your persuasive communication more effective.

Let's talk about body language first. Your audience's perception of your message can be greatly influenced by your body language. You can make your message more persuasive and clear by paying attention to your body language.

Posture is a crucial component of body language. With your shoulders back and your head held high, stand straight.

This will not only enable you to breathe more deeply, which can help to calm your nerves and improve your delivery, but it will also help you to project confidence.

Eye contact is another crucial aspect of body language. Throughout your presentation, be sure to make eye contact with your audience frequently. You can gain your audience's trust and establish a connection by doing this.

Another crucial component of body language is gestures. Make use of organic, emotive gestures to support your arguments and reaffirm your message. Avoid nervous or fidgety movements, which can divert attention from your point.

Let's now talk about voice. Another crucial weapon for successful communication is your voice. You may improve the impact and efficacy of your message by developing your voice.

Tone is a crucial component of voice. To build credibility and convey authority, adopt a confident, authoritative tone. Change your tone to emphasize points and express feelings when necessary.

Pace is a key component of voice as well. Talk slowly and pause sometimes to let your audience process what you're saying. Avoid speaking too hastily since your listeners may find it challenging to follow along.

Next, be sure to project your voice forcefully and clearly so that your audience can hear you. If necessary, use a microphone to make sure that everyone in the room hears what you have to say.

You may improve the impact of your persuasive communication and raise the probability that your audience will be persuaded by developing your body language and voice.

We will go over some important tactics for dealing with challenging queries and objections from your audience in the following chapter.

It can be beneficial to rehearse in front of a mirror or videotape yourself giving a presentation in order to improve your body language and voice. You can then pay attention to and modify your posture, gestures, tone, and tempo.

Along with practicing alone, think about asking a trusted friend or mentor to give you feedback on your voice and body language. You may improve your communication abilities and pinpoint any areas that need work by doing this.

It's crucial to keep in mind that your voice and body language should match your message. Your body language and voice should reflect the confidence and authority you are trying to express with your words. Your message may come across less clearly if your verbal and nonverbal communication are inconsistent.

Finally, remember that interpersonal communication relies heavily on body language and voice in addition to being crucial for public speaking.

You may improve your communication abilities in all facets of your life, from formal presentations to casual chats, by developing your body language and voice.

Another essential competency for effective persuasive communication is how to respond to challenging queries and objections from your audience, which will be covered in the following chapter.

Preparation is essential when dealing with challenging queries and objections from your audience. Have a strategy in place for answering any queries and rebuttals that your audience may have.

Rephrasing the objection as a question is one tactic. For instance, if someone objects to your suggestion, you could respond by asking, "Interesting point, I agree. Could you elaborate on the reasons behind your feelings?" This strategy enables you to comprehend the objection more fully and can ease any anxiety.

Another tactic is to accept the criticism and offer a refutation. Say, "I understand your concern, but let me explain why I believe this idea is still the greatest alternative." as an illustration. This strategy reinforces your own stance while demonstrating to your audience that you are paying attention to them and are willing to discuss their issues.

Also, it's critical to maintain composure and composure when responding to challenging queries and arguments.

Breathe deeply and keep in mind that it's normal for folks to have queries and worries. You may assist in defusing any possible disputes and upholding the authority of your message by acting in a respectful and professional manner.

Last but not least, be sure to address any queries or criticisms that you were unable to fully address throughout your presentation. This can help to generate trust and foster a good relationship with your audience by demonstrating your commitment to communicating with them and responding to their issues.

You can improve the effectiveness of your persuasive communication and make sure that your audience hears and understands your message by becoming an expert at managing challenging inquiries and objections.

CHAPTER 10

CREATING COMPELLING VISUALS

A key component of persuasion is the creation of captivating pictures. Using visual aids can help you strengthen your points, engage your audience, and make difficult concepts easier to understand.

It's crucial to take your audience's wants and preferences into account while developing images. Which kind of visual assistance will best help you make your point? Will a diagram, chart, or graph be more impactful than a picture or example?

Also, it's crucial to make sure that your pictures are understandable and crystal clear. Refrain from using cluttered or overly complicated pictures that could confuse or overwhelm your viewers.

Make sure that your images are the right size for the space and the audience by choosing colors and fonts that are both easy to read and aesthetically pleasing.

Consider employing dynamic graphics, such as movies or animations, in addition to static images, to engage your audience and improve their comprehension of your content.
These images can be very useful for explaining difficult ideas or procedures.

It's crucial to effortlessly incorporate graphics into your presentation when employing them to convey your point. In order to avoid detracting from your vocal communication, make sure your images enhance and support it. To draw attention to important details and keep your audience interested throughout your presentation, use your visuals carefully.

Last but not least, keep in mind that graphics are simply one weapon in your toolbox for effective communication. They can be powerful, but they should be used with other persuasive techniques like fascinating storytelling and good verbal communication.

You can improve the effectiveness of your persuasive communication and make sure that your audience hears and understands your message by developing the skill of producing appealing images.

Using data visualization techniques is one way to provide visually appealing content. For instance, charts and graphs can be used to convey complex data sets in a way that is clear and pleasing to the eye.

Yet, it's crucial to pick the appropriate type of graph or chart for the information you're presenting. A line graph may be superior for displaying trends over time whereas a bar graph may be more useful for comparing data.

Accessibility is a crucial factor while developing visuals. Make sure that everyone in your audience, including those who are color-blind or have visual impairments, can access your visuals. To help guarantee that your graphics are accessible to everyone, take into consideration employing high-contrast colors and including alternate text descriptions.

Less is frequently more when it comes to images. A slide or presentation should not have too many graphics; doing so can overwhelm your audience and make it harder for them to concentrate on your topic. Instead, pick a few standout graphics that can strengthen your ideas and enhance your message.

Finally, don't be scared to try out various graphic formats and presentation techniques. You might find fresh, cutting-edge ways to engage your audience and express your message as you get more experienced making pictures. The secret is to keep an open mind and be eager to explore new things.

You can advance your persuasive communication abilities and make sure that your audience hears and understands your message by becoming an expert in the creation of engaging graphics.

You may improve the impact of your presentations and speeches by becoming a skilled visual communicator with practice and perseverance.

CHAPTER 11

HANDLING OBJECTIONS AND RESISTANCE.

Handling objections and opposition from your audience is one of the most difficult components of persuasive communication.

Even the most skillfully constructed and persuasive argument could run against resistance from some audience members. Yet, by anticipating objections and reacting to them thoughtfully and constructively, you can allay your audience's worries and improve the likelihood that your message will be understood.

Being prepared for objections is a crucial tactic for dealing with them. Consider the most frequent criticisms that your audience is likely to voice, then create responses that address these issues.

For instance, you might need to address concerns about the venture's possible dangers and uncertainties if you're seeking to convince a group of investors to fund your firm.

You may boost your credibility and win your audience's trust by anticipating these arguments and creating responses that recognise and resolve these worries.

Maintaining composure and concentration when responding to critiques or pushback is another crucial component in handling concerns. It's crucial to pay close attention to your audience's worries and to refrain from getting defensive or combative. Instead, take the effort to comprehend their viewpoint and make a positive, courteous response.

The "feel, felt, found" method is a helpful foundation for responding to objections. This entails expressing an understanding of the other person's worry ("I know how you feel"), identifying with it ("I've felt that way before, too"), and then responding to it ("What I've found is that...").

This tactic can help you establish connection with your audience, win their trust, and show them that you are paying attention to their worries.

To counter criticisms, it's also a good idea to back up your claims with examples and supporting proof. To show the efficacy and impact of your message, use data, statistics, and case studies.

This can assist allay doubts that others may have regarding the viability or usefulness of your idea and boost their trust in your message.

In the end, maintaining flexibility and adaptability will help you deal with complaints and opposition. Be ready to modify your message or strategy in response to audience input, and have an open mind to suggestions and constructive criticism.

By doing this, you can enhance the likelihood that your persuasive communication attempts will be successful by gaining the audience's confidence and credibility.

There are a few other methods and recommendations that might assist you deal with objections and resistance from your audience in addition to the approaches outlined above.

Using "the power of why" is a crucial strategy. This entails asking insightful questions to assist your audience in comprehending the fundamental causes of their protests or resistance.

By asking questions like "Why do you feel that way?" or "Can you help me comprehend your concerns more fully?", you can engage your audience in a dialogue and obtain a deeper grasp of their perspective. This can assist you in addressing their issues more efficiently and establishing a more cooperative and fruitful rapport with your audience.

A further effective tactic is to offer background and viewpoint. Often misunderstandings or poor communication are the root cause of objections or resistance.

Your audience can better understand your message and the reasoning behind it if you provide more context or background information. For instance, if some coworkers object to your suggestion of a new policy at work, you might wish to elaborate on the rationale behind the proposal as well as any prospective advantages.

keep in mind that challenges and opposition might present chances for development and education.

You can determine areas where you might need to change your message or strategy by actively listening to the complaints and suggestions of your audience.

Consider how you can apply the feedback you get to your upcoming communication efforts after giving it some thought.

You can deal with resistance and objections successfully by employing these strategies and techniques, which will also help your persuasive communication efforts be more successful. Keep in mind to maintain composure, mental openness, and flexibility as you respond to audience feedback. You may develop your communication skills and ability to influence even the most resistant audiences with effort and practice.

Anticipating objections and opposition in advance is a useful strategy for dealing with them. Consider any potential objections or worries your audience may have before you deliver a presentation or make a pitch.

Take into account their viewpoint and make an effort to understand what they are thinking. This can assist you in locating potential obstacles and creating plans for dealing with them.

Also, it's critical to acknowledge your audience's issues and actively listen to them. Even if you disagree with their points, you should recognize them and demonstrate that you understand them.

This can support the development of trust and the creation of a more satisfying and fruitful relationship with your audience.

Using facts and proof to back up your claims is another effective strategy. You are more likely to persuade your audience that your message is true if you can back it up with specific instances, figures, or other forms of proof.

Use reliable sources, and present the data in a way that is both persuasive and straightforward.

CHAPTER 12

STRATEGIES FOR ADDRESSING SKEPTICISM AND DOUBT

Anyone trying to persuade their audience needs to have methods for dealing with skepticism and uncertainty.

If the listener has qualms or doubts about the speaker or the message, even the strongest arguments may fall flat. The following are some sensible responses to skepticism and uncertainty:

One of the best strategies for combating skepticism and doubt is to acknowledge and respond to any worries your audience might have. You might address this immediately by highlighting your credentials or experience if your audience has any reservations about your legitimacy.

You could answer any doubts about your proposal's viability or applicability by giving specific examples or case studies.

Use Social Proof: The concept of social proof holds that people are more likely to accept a claim as true if they observe others doing so.

Using social proof to dispel skepticism and doubt is a useful strategy. You can achieve this by emphasizing recommendations or reviews from pleased clients, as well as by referencing data or research to back up your assertions.

Develop Relationships: Another successful strategy for dealing with skepticism and doubt is to develop relationships with your audience.

People are more likely to believe and trust someone when they sense a personal connection with them. By being approachable, interesting, and relatable, you may develop rapport.

Finding similar ground with your audience, using comedy, or sharing personal tales can all help you establish rapport.

Employ Emotion: Emotions are an effective persuasion tool. You are more likely to influence your audience if you can appeal to their emotions. You may utilize tales or illustrations that make people feel something, whether it's excitement, astonishment, or inspiration. Nonetheless, it's critical to avoid deceptive techniques and use emotions in a genuine and authentic way.

Handle Counterarguments: Directly responding to counter arguments is another powerful strategy for dispelling skepticism and uncertainty.

You can showcase your knowledge and experience while also displaying that you are open to many opinions if you can foresee and answer probable objections or alternative viewpoints. With your audience, this can support the development of credibility and trust.

These techniques will help you deal with skepticism and doubt and improve your ability to persuade your audience. It's crucial to keep in mind, though, that persuasion is not about controlling or deceiving people.

It's all about connecting with your audience on a real level by communicating your thoughts in a clear, captivating, and genuine manner.

Using social proof is another tactic for combating skepticism and doubt. The idea of social proof holds that people are more inclined to take a particular activity if they observe others doing the same thing.

Because it appeals to people's innate need to fit in and belong to a group, this has the potential to be especially persuasive.

You can utilize examples of people who have already taken the desired action in your persuasive communication to employ social proof.

This can entail presenting case studies or customer reviews, revealing data on the amount of people who have actually engaged in the behavior, or even displaying images or videos of actual users or beneficiaries of the good or service.

Using the influence of thought leaders or influencers in your sector is another approach to use social proof. These are people who are well-liked and esteemed in their industry.

A thought leader's or influencer's endorsement of your good or service can go a long way toward persuading others to act.

It's crucial to remember that social proof should only be applied in genuine, ethical ways. Verify that any testimonials you use are genuine and weren't created by you.

Also, if you're using thought leaders or influencers, make sure they support your product or service truly and aren't just being paid to promote it.

By providing evidence that others have already performed the desired action and experienced success, you can use social proof as a persuasive approach to assist people get over skepticism and doubt. Your audience may feel more secure and at ease as a result, which increases the likelihood that they will perform the required action.

Using the reciprocity principle is another method for combating skepticism and uncertainty. According to the principle of reciprocity, we have a moral obligation to repay kindness when it is shown to us.

This suggests that, in the context of persuasive communication, if you can give your audience something helpful before asking them to do anything, they could be more inclined to respond by doing that item.

You may offer your audience something of value that is associated with your good or service in order to put the reciprocity principle into practice.

You may offer your audience a complimentary manual on overcoming stage fear, for instance, if you're offering a course on public speaking.

By giving them something of value up front, you may show them that you care about their success and aren't just out to make a sale.

Offering a free trial or sample of your good or service is another approach to put the rule of reciprocity to action.

This increases the likelihood that your audience will make a purchase or take the necessary action by enabling them to personally experience the value of your service.

It's critical to keep in mind that the reciprocity principle does not ensure success. It's crucial to give something genuine and sincere in exchange.

Your chances of influencing your audience may be harmed if you come out as manipulative or disingenuous.

CHAPTER 13

THE ROLE OF ETHICS IN PERSUASION

A strong weapon for influencing others and achieving one's objectives is persuasion. But with tremendous power comes great responsibility, so it's critical to think about how persuasion could affect morality.

The art of persuasion is frequently linked to psychological manipulation of people's attitudes and actions in order to bring about a desired result.

This can be seen in politics, commerce, and advertising, where persuasion is frequently used to persuade people to purchase a good, back a cause, or cast a ballot for a particular person. Yet, if it involves manipulation, coercion, or fraud, this form of persuasion may be unethical.

It's critical to respect other people's rights and dignity if you want to engage in ethical persuasion. This means that any statements made should be backed up by evidence and that the material supplied should be accurate and true.

Fear, intimidation, or coercion should not be used in the process of persuasion, and it should be done with respect for the person's autonomy and freedom of choice.

Ethical persuasion entails being sincere and respectful, as well as taking into account how one's actions will affect others in the future. In other words, the persuader needs to be mindful of how their argument might affect a person, a group, or the environment. It is unethical to persuade in a way that causes harm or damage to any of these areas.

A perspective of empathy and understanding can be used to assure ethical persuasion. This entails paying attention to the requirements, preferences, and viewpoints of the person being convinced and adjusting the message accordingly.

By doing this, the persuader can win the person's trust and establish a connection with them, increasing the likelihood that they will be open to the message.

The examination of cultural and social norms is a crucial component of ethical persuasion. Because values and ideas vary among nations and societies, what may be compelling in one setting may not be in another.

The persuader needs to be aware of these variations and modify their strategy accordingly.

Using the art of persuasion responsibly can help one achieve their goals and be a strong tool. In order to persuade someone ethically, one must respect their rights and dignity, provide information truthfully and accurately, evaluate the long-term effects of one's actions, approach the person with empathy and compassion, and be conscious of cultural and societal standards.

By engaging in ethical persuasion, we can create connections based on trust, advance our objectives, and do so with upholding our moral principles and regard for others.

It's crucial to keep in mind that the techniques by which you accomplish that aim can have ethical repercussions, even while the ultimate purpose of persuasion is to persuade your audience to do a specific action or adopt a certain opinion.

Persuasion is fundamentally about influencing others through speech, and this ability can be exercised both constructively and destructively. So, it is crucial to think about the ethical consequences of your persuasive strategies and make sure you are employing them in a responsible and ethically acceptable manner.

Transparency is a key component of ethical persuasion. Being upfront and truthful about your objectives is vital when attempting to persuade someone.

This entails being open and honest about any prejudices or conflicts of interest you may have and refraining from misleading or manipulating your audience.

It's important to disclose any financial incentives or sponsorships that might be affecting your endorsement, for instance, if you're pushing a specific product.

Respecting the autonomy of your audience is a crucial ethical factor. Coercion or manipulation that impairs a person's capacity to make a free and informed decision should never be used in the course of persuasion. Hence, it's critical to refrain from utilizing strategies that could unfairly influence someone's decision-making process, such as creating fear, manipulating emotions, or applying pressure.

Last but not least, ethical persuasion calls for a dedication to justice and fairness. This entails being aware of and considerate of the viewpoints and requirements of others who might be impacted by your persuasive messages as well as making an effort to ensure that your arguments are supported by reliable data and sound reasoning.

It also entails being open to contemplating different thoughts and perspectives and willing to participate in respectful discourse and debate.

Understanding that persuasion is a type of power and that it has major ethical duties, like all forms of power, is ultimately the key to ethical persuasion.

You may make sure that your persuasive messages are not only powerful but also morally and responsibly by embracing openness, respecting autonomy, and committing to fairness and justice.

CHAPTER 14

PRESENTING A COMPELLING PRESENTATION.

Making a Convincing Presentation

The critical next step after creating a powerful message is effectively communicating it to your audience.

Excellent delivery is essential to the success of any message. Your chances of persuading your audience to accept your message might be improved or hampered by how you deliver it. Hence, it is crucial that you convey your point with conviction, clarity, and assurance.

These are some pointers for making a convincing presentation:

Know your material
It's important to be well familiar with your subject matter. This entails having a thorough understanding of your message, your target audience, and the evidence you want to utilize to support your assertions.

Understanding your content inside and out will make it easier for you to present with confidence because you won't need to refer to your notes or slides as much.

Strongly begin.

The tone of your presentation can be established with a powerful introduction. Start your presentation with a stunning fact, a perplexing query, or an impactful narrative to capture the interest of your audience. Make the most of this chance to engage your audience and build trust.

Speak eloquently and with passion

Your delivery is just as crucial as the information in your presentation. Keep your audience interested by speaking with confidence and excitement.

To emphasize your points, use body language, facial emotions, and gestures. Ensure that everyone in the room can plainly hear you by raising your voice.

Employ tales and examples

People are more likely to relate to stories and instances than to facts and figures. To demonstrate your arguments and help your audience relate to your message, use pertinent anecdotes and examples.

Effectively utilize images to help your audience comprehend your content. Utilize graphs, charts, and pictures to illustrate your arguments, but watch out for over-visualizing your presentation. Employ only the visuals that are required to successfully communicate your message.

Consider any objections your audience may have before you deliver your message in order to prepare for them.

In your presentation, address these criticisms and offer arguments in opposition. With your audience, this will assist establish credibility and trust.

Strong call to action at the conclusion of your presentation will motivate your audience to take action.

Have a clear path for your audience to follow and make it obvious what you want them to do. Long after your presentation is ended, your audience will still remember your message thanks to this.

Giving a persuasive presentation necessitates the utilization of strong information, assured delivery, and impactful images.

By putting these suggestions to use, you may engage your audience, establish your credibility, and improve your odds of getting them to act.

Always remember that practice makes perfect, so practice your presentation before the big event and ask for comments to help you give it better.

Even though you've worked hard to create a compelling message and ready your pictures, your work isn't yet done. You must convey your message with conviction, fervor, and confidence if you want to completely win over your audience.

Start off well

The tone of your presentation is established at the outset. Start off with a strong hook that seizes the attention of your audience and draws them into your message right away. To engage your audience, you might utilize a captivating statistic, an interesting personal experience, or a thought-provoking query.

Talk with Confidence

Your audience's perception of your message will be greatly influenced by your body language, tone of voice, and general manner. A clear, confident tone of voice and a straight posture are important when speaking. Don't use unnecessary words like "uh" and "like," which can hurt your credibility.

Employ Powerful Language

You need to use powerful language to really connect with your audience. Employ sensory-engaging language to assist your audience visualize what you're trying to say. Steer clear of technical or jargon-filled language that could mislead your viewers.

Efficient Usage of Visual Aids

Your visual aids should support rather than detract from your message. Employ graphics that clearly and simply illustrate your primary arguments. Limit the amount of information on your slides, and make sure to explain each image thoroughly.

No matter how captivating your message is, there will inevitably be some people in your audience who may have questions or reservations.

Consider these criticisms and be ready to respond to them in your presentation. This establishes your credibility with your audience and demonstrates that you have thought critically about all options.

The ultimate objective of any persuasive presentation is to persuade your audience to act. Clarify what you want your audience to do and how they can do it, whether it's signing a petition, making a gift, or altering their behavior.

The final component of presenting a persuasive presentation is practice: practice, practice, practice. Practice your speech numerous times; ideally, do it in front of a friend or work colleague who can offer suggestions.

To make sure you can properly communicate your message, practice speaking clearly and confidently, and concentrate on tempo and timing.

You'll be well on your way to making a powerful presentation that engages your audience and inspires action by paying attention to these pointers.

Always remember that having a clear, compelling message that connects with your audience as well as preparation and confidence are the keys to success.

CHAPTER 15

ENGAGING YOUR AUDIENCE AND INSPIRING ACTION

The ultimate objectives of any persuasive presentation are to engage your audience and motivate them to take action.

It's crucial to establish a connection with your audience and give them a reason to believe in your message if you want to accomplish these goals.

Some effective methods for reaching this objective include the following:

Activate their interest

Getting your audience's attention at the start of your presentation is essential. You can use a variety of strategies to get your point over quickly, including a strong opening statement, an eye-popping statistic, or a gripping narrative that introduces your topic.

Speak the native tongue

Employ words that your audience will understand. Avoid using buzzwords and technical language that they might not understand. Use language that is simple to understand and that reflects their views and values instead.

Be comprehensible Provide personal tales or anecdotes that will resonate with your audience. Make it apparent that you are not just preaching to them and that you comprehend their point of view.

Employ comedy

Using humor can help to reduce tension and break down boundaries. To lighten the mood and create a pleasant environment for your audience, use suitable comedy.

Make emotional connections since they are effective motivators. Employ narratives, visuals, and language that arouse powerful feelings like empathy, compassion, or hope.

Make it participatory

Engage your audience by posing inquiries, promoting dialogue, or even introducing games or other activities that help to clarify your point.

Use visuals

Visual aids can strengthen and increase the recall of your message. To further support your argument, provide infographics, videos, and/or photographs.

Your compelling presentation should conclude with a call to action because that is what it is ultimately intended to do.

Clearly state what action you want your audience to do and why it is necessary. By giving them specific instructions they can follow, motivate them to take action.

You may engage your audience and motivate them to act by utilizing these techniques. Recall that engaging your audience and instilling a sense of ownership in them are essential components of an effective presentation.

CHAPTER 16

MESSAGES CREATION FOR MAXIMUM IMPACT

The key to effective persuasion is developing a message that connects with your audience. But how can you create a message that really gets the point across and inspires people to act? The fundamental ideas underlying crafting a message that inspires, engages, and persuades will be covered in this chapter.

Recognize Your Audience

Knowing your target is the first step in creating a persuasive message. They, who? Why do they do it? What do they believe and value? Your message must be customized to meet their requirements, wants, and expectations. By researching your audience, you may learn about their problems, obstacles, and goals.

This might assist you in crafting a message that relates to their priorities and areas of interest.

Create a Strong and Clear Message

After gaining an understanding of your audience, you must create a message that is captivating and resonant with them. This entails finding the key advantages of your concept, product, or service and structuring them in a manner that appeals to the requirements and wants of your target market.

A excellent message need to be uncomplicated, unambiguous, and remembered. It should be simple to comprehend and explain. Your message will be more difficult for people to understand and remember if it is more complicated.

Utilize convincing language

When it comes to persuasion, words matter. The words you use can significantly affect how your message is understood. In order to be persuasive, one must use words and phrases that evoke strong feelings and motivate action.

Positive language can, for instance, be more powerful than negative language. Concentrate on the solutions rather than the issues. Consider using adjectives like "opportunity," "creative," and "revolutionary" when describing your good or service. This may contribute to generating excitement and enthusiasm.

Share a Story

Storytelling is one of the most effective techniques to engage your audience and win them over to your point of view. People can be drawn in by stories and have their emotions stirred. People can comprehend your message more deeply when you use a good narrative.

Always keep your tale pertinent to your point in mind when sharing it. Employ relatable characters, situations, and storylines to engage your audience. A good story ought to be interesting, educational, and memorable.

Employ social proof

If they perceive that others are following the message, people are more likely to do the same. We call this social proof. By citing instances of other people who have profited from your product, service, or concept, you can use social proof to your advantage.

To demonstrate how your product, service, or concept has benefited others, for instance, you can utilize testimonies, case studies, and statistics. Your argument may be stronger as a result of building credibility and trust.

Final Reflections

A persuasive message must be carefully thought out, planned, and delivered. You may design a message that genuinely resonates with your audience and motivates action by knowing your audience, generating a clear and appealing message, using persuasive language, telling a captivating tale, and utilizing social proof.

Keep in mind that a persuasive message should focus on developing real relationships with people that are founded on empathy, trust, and understanding rather than on deceiving or manipulating them.

The most crucial phase in persuasion is carefully constructing your message in order to influence your audience.

You must convey your idea or argument in a way that connects with your audience and inspires them to act if you want to persuade them to act.

The way you structure your message can make the difference between success and failure, whether you're giving a speech, preparing a paper, or pitching a product.

Your audience should be one of the first factors taken into account while developing your message. What do they care about and who are they? What drives them, as well as what are their wants and needs? By using language and examples that are pertinent to and related to the group you are speaking to, you should customize your message for that audience. You'll have a better chance of winning them over if you can address their issues and relate to their values.

The benefits of your proposal or idea should be identified and highlighted as a crucial component of any compelling message.

This entails emphasizing the advantages that your audience will experience if they follow your recommendations.

You must demonstrate your audience how your product or concept will improve their lives or solve their issues, rather than just listing its characteristics. Examples from real life, data, and testimonies can all be used to demonstrate this.

Together with emphasizing advantages, it's crucial to address any potential objections or worries your audience may have. You can gain your audience's trust and credibility by anticipating and responding to objections beforehand.

This entails identifying any potential drawbacks and restrictions and proving that the advantages outweigh them. By doing this, you can demonstrate to your audience that you are actually concerned for their welfare rather than just trying to sell them something.

Using language that is crystal clear, succinct, and convincing is another essential component of creating a persuasive message. This entails staying away from jargon and technical language that could perplex or alienate your readers in favor of utilizing straightforward, understandable terms. It also entails utilizing expressive language that piques interest and elicits strong feelings.

You can increase the impact and recall of your message by employing metaphors, anecdotes, and other rhetorical techniques.

The process of creating a persuasive message is iterative, so keep that in mind as well. Based on feedback from your audience and actual outcomes, you might need to test and improve your message over time.

This entails being receptive to helpful criticism and feedback and prepared to modify your strategy as necessary. Everyone can learn to create a message that actually resonates with their audience and motivates action if they are persistent, creative, and open to learning new things.

CHAPTER 17

OVERCOMING OPPOSITION AND OBJECTIONS

It's usual for an audience to reject or oppose yoursn message in the world of persuasion. Overcoming these obstacles is a crucial ability for every persuasive communicator, regardless of whether they are brought on by preconceived conceptions, personal views, or lack of interest.

Predicting objections before they occur is one of the best methods to deal with them. To do this, you must comprehend your audience and any prospective issues. By putting yourself in their position, you may modify your message to fully address their worries and remove any potential objections.

The ability to reframe concerns as opportunities is another effective tactic. See criticisms as chances to resolve issues and forge deeper connections with your audience rather than as barriers to your message.

By recognizing objections and promptly responding to them, you show empathy and understanding, which can increase trust and, ultimately, your persuasiveness.

Also, it's critical to keep in mind that emotional rather than logical concerns frequently underlie arguments. This means that using your audience's emotions as a weapon to overcome objections can be very effective. For instance, if a member of the audience is opposed to a certain policy out of worry for their family, structuring your argument in a way that appeals to their care can help you override that resistance.

Making advantage of social proof is another successful tactic. People prefer to take the thoughts and actions of others around them at face value, so if you can show that others have accepted your message or solution, it can help to dispel doubts and gain traction.

Last but not least, never undervalue the power of perseverance. It frequently takes several attempts and constant communication to overcome obstacles. Don't give up if a viewer rejects your point of view. Talk to them more, pay attention to what they have to say, and try to find something in common. Even the most resistant audience members can be won over with time and effort.

Overcoming audience resistance and objections is one of the toughest obstacles in persuasive communication.

Objections and resistance can take many different forms, such as skepticism about your authority, disapproval of your message, or worries about the possible repercussions of adopting the course of action you recommend.

Recognizing and openly addressing concerns and resistance is the key to getting through them. Ignoring or dismissing issues will only make your audience feel unheard and decrease their likelihood of being persuaded.

It's crucial to foresee objections and opposition in order to successfully handle them. Prepare responses in advance to any potential objections or worries your audience may have.

This will enable you to address them before they arise and show that you've considered the possible effects of your message.

It's crucial to respond to objections and resistance in a respectful and sympathetic manner. Demonstrate your audience that you appreciate their viewpoint and are receptive to their worries. Building rapport and trust in this way will make it more likely that your message will be received favorably in the long run.

Using social evidence is a successful tactic for overcoming objections and opposition. Using examples or testimonies from those who have successfully completed the action you're recommending is known as social proof.

This can assuage worries and provide evidence that similar actions have produced favorable results in the past.

Use of reframing is another tactic. Reframing entails taking a criticism or worry and viewing it from a different angle.

If someone is worried about the price of a good or service, for instance, you may reframe the conversation by emphasizing the long-term advantages and potential cost savings of adopting the suggested action.

When encountering objections or resistance, it's also crucial to refrain from being defensive or argumentative. Instead, keep your composure, be considerate of others, and concentrate on connecting with your audience.

This will assist in keeping the discussion on track and concentrated on coming up with a solution that benefits everyone.

In the end, the secret to overcoming objections and resistance is to pay attention to your audience and show that you care about their wants and needs. By doing this, you can enhance the likelihood that your message will be accepted favorably and put into action by your audience. You can also develop trust and rapport with them.

Overcoming objections and resistance is an essential part of persuasion. You can boost your persuasive power and motivate your audience to take action by anticipating objections, presenting them as opportunities, appealing to emotions, employing social evidence, and remaining persistent in your efforts.

CHAPTER 18

PRESENTING A COMPELLING PRESENTATION: THE COMPLETE GUIDE

It's time to present your convincing message to your audience after careful planning, investigation, and drafting. When you successfully engage your audience and motivate them to take action, all of your hard work will have been worthwhile.

The tactics and methods for making a convincing presentation that is interesting, memorable, and powerful will be covered in this chapter.

Practice and Rehearse

It's crucial to practice and rehearse your presentation before taking the stage. This will make your material more familiar to you and ensure that you convey your message clearly.

Get a friend or coworker to listen to and provide criticism while you practice your delivery in front of a mirror, record yourself, and then watch it back.

Establishing a connection with your audience is essential to presenting a captivating presentation.

Start by making eye contact, using nice body language, and developing a connection with them. To engage them and make your presentation relevant to their needs and interests, use examples, tales, and comedy.

Employ Visual Aids

Using slides, charts, and movies as visual aids will help you communicate your point more clearly and keep your audience interested.

Make sure your visual aids are crystal clear, succinct, and eye-catching. Use as few visual aids as possible; too many might become overpowering and detract from your message.

Use Emotional Appeals

Emotions are a strong persuasion weapon. To captivate your audience and establish an emotional connection with them, use emotional appeals.

Employ tales and illustrations that cause people to feel empathy, excitement, or fear. To prevent overusing emotional appeals, make sure that they are pertinent to your argument.

Handling Objections

Delivering a persuasive presentation requires that you address Objections. Be prepared to respond to frequent concerns and objections that your audience may raise.

Demonstrate understanding and compassion, and to refute arguments, offer data and examples. To make your argument and demonstrate how your message might allay their anxieties, use tales and anecdotes.

Call to Action

A call to action should always be included at the end of a powerful presentation. Following hearing your message, you want your audience to do this.

Describe the action you want them to take in clear, succinct terms, and make sure it relates to your message. To motivate your audience to act, use stories and emotional appeals.

After giving your presentation, give yourself some time to reflect on it and make any necessary improvements. Examine audience input to find areas that need improvement. Incorporate improvements into your delivery, messaging, and visual aids. Make use of this criticism to strengthen your future speeches and hone your persuasion skills.

Making a persuasive presentation requires careful planning, excellent delivery, and knowledge of the requirements and interests of your audience.

You can deliver a persuading presentation that motivates action by practicing and rehearsing, engaging with your audience, utilizing visual aids, emotional appeals, and resolving objections.

Always remember to leave your audience with a clear call to action, and always be looking for ways to improve. You may improve your speaking skills and leave an impression on your audience by using these methods and strategies.

When making a persuasive presentation that truly connects with your audience, there are a few crucial components to keep in mind in addition to the advice and tactics covered previously in this book. Consider the following supplementary information:

Practice, practice, practice

It might sound obvious, but the best approach to deliver an effective presentation is to regularly practice it until you feel assured and at ease with the subject matter.

This will prevent you from tripping over your words or losing your position when you speak, allowing you to concentrate on connecting with your audience and effectively conveying your message.

Recognize your audience

Spend some time getting to know your audience before you deliver your presentation. What are their wants, passions, and worries? Why do they do it? Use words and situations that they can relate to, and personalize your message to their particular circumstance.

Start off strong

Your opening words are important for grabbing the attention of your audience and bringing them into your presentation. To break the ice and build a connection with your listeners, begin with a riveting anecdote or statistic, pose a challenging question, or utilize humor.

Utilize visual tools to help demonstrate your arguments and keep your audience interested. Visual aids include presentations, diagrams, and movies.

However, take care not to rely on them excessively because you don't want to divert attention from your message or saturate your audience with information.

Employ persuasive body language

Your nonverbal communication can be just as powerful as your spoken one. To accentuate your ideas and show your audience that you are passionate about your subject, stand up straight, create eye contact with them, and use gestures and your facial emotions.

Discuss any concerns Face any objections or worries that your audience may have head-on and address them in your presentation.

This will show that you have given the situation due consideration from all angles and will help to establish credibility and confidence.

Your ultimate objective is to motivate your audience to act in response to your message, therefore end with a call to action.

Make sure to conclude your speech with a strong call to action, whether it is to give money to a cause, sign a petition, or just to consider an issue more carefully.

You may produce a persuading presentation that really connects with your audience and motivates them to act by heeding these suggestions, putting in the necessary preparation, and making the necessary effort.

Recall that persuasion is a skill that can be learned by anyone; it is both an art and a science.

CHAPTER 19

KEY STRATEGIES FOR FOLLOWING UP WITH YOUR AUDIENCE AFTER YOUR COMMUNICATION

Effective communication continues after your presentation or message has been delivered. To make sure that your message is heard and comprehended, you must check in with your audience.

The possibility of future opportunities can be increased and long-term connections can be strengthened with the use of a follow-up approach.

The following are some essential tactics for engaging your audience after your communication:

Prepare your follow-up in advance by considering the goals for it before you even deliver your message. Choose the best follow-up strategy, whether it be a phone call, email, or in-person encounter.

Establish a timetable for your follow-up and decide what data you'll need to get from your audience to figure out what to do next.

Customize your follow-up

Address each member of your audience specifically in your follow-up communications. Make reference to particular areas that were covered in your communication and tailor your follow-up message to their individual requirements and interests. This special touch demonstrates your appreciation for their time and care.

Provide more informational materials Include supplementary materials, such as articles, research, or case studies, that bolster your argument.
These sources can support your points and offer more information on the subject at hand.

Invite your audience to offer feedback on your presentation or message by making a request for it. You can use feedback to identify problem areas and make improvements to future communications.

Identify future steps

Give your viewers clear instructions regarding how to proceed. Organizing a product demonstration, organizing a follow-up meeting, or sending further information for evaluation are examples of how to do this.

Outlining the following steps succinctly keeps the dialogue on track and prevents any misunderstandings.

Follow up promptly

When it comes to follow-up, time is of the essence. To make sure that your message is still fresh in your audience's mind, aim to follow up within 24-48 hours following your conversation. If you wait too long, your audience may forget what you said or lose interest.

Keep the connection going

Getting in touch with your audience thereafter gives you a chance to develop and deepen your connections.

By sending out regular updates, sharing news from the business, or providing insightful commentary, stay in touch with your audience. By doing so, you may be able to keep them interested in your message and raise the possibility of subsequent possibilities.

The right kind of follow-up can help you hone your message and fortify your connections with your audience. You can make sure that your message is heard and understood by pre-planning your follow-up, customizing your communication, and offering extra resources.

CONCLUSION

THE POWER OF PERSUASION IN TODAY'S WORLD

The art of persuasion is a timeless skill that has been used throughout history to influence people, inspire change, and achieve success.

In today's world, where communication and influence are critical, mastering the art of persuasion is more important than ever.

Whether you are a business leader, a salesperson, a teacher, a politician, or anyone who wants to be more persuasive, the strategies and techniques outlined in this book can help you achieve your goals.

Throughout this book, we have explored the various elements that make up effective persuasion, from understanding the psychology of persuasion to building credibility and trust, framing your message, using emotional appeals, mastering nonverbal communication, and creating compelling visuals.

We have also looked at strategies for handling objections, addressing skepticism and doubt, and using storytelling to make your message more engaging and memorable.

But the art of persuasion is not just about the techniques and strategies; it's also about the ethical considerations that come with influencing others. In today's world, where trust and authenticity are more important than ever, it's crucial to use persuasion in a way that is honest, transparent, and respectful of others' beliefs and values.

Ultimately, the goal of persuasion is not just to convince people to do something but to inspire them to take action.

Whether you want to sell a product, promote a cause, or persuade people to adopt a new way of thinking, the key is to engage your audience and make them feel invested in your message.

By understanding what motivates your audience, tailoring your message to their needs and interests, and using storytelling and other persuasive techniques to create an emotional connection, you can inspire them to take action and achieve your goals.

The power of persuasion is undeniable in today's world. By mastering the art of persuasion, you can achieve your goals, inspire positive change, and make a lasting impact on the world around you.

Remember, effective communication and the ability to influence others are skills that can be learned and honed over time. With dedication and practice, anyone can become a persuasive communicator and achieve their dreams.